CLASS 91 LOCOMOTIVES

Andrew Cole

AMBERLEY

First published 2018

Amberley Publishing
The Hill, Stroud
Gloucestershire, GL5 4EP

www.amberley-books.com

Copyright © Andrew Cole, 2018

The right of Andrew Cole to be identified as
the Author of this work has been asserted in
accordance with the Copyrights, Designs and
Patents Act 1988.

ISBN 978 1 4456 8137 5 (print)
ISBN 978 1 4456 8138 2 (ebook)

British Library Cataloguing in Publication Data.
A catalogue record for this book is available from
the British Library.

Origination by Amberley Publishing.
Printed in the UK.

Introduction

The Class 91 locomotives were constructed at BREL Crewe Works from 1988 onwards, with a total of thirty-one being built. Designed by GEC, the build work was sub-contracted to BREL, and the locos were known as Electras throughout their construction.

They were built for use on the East Coast Main Line, linking London King's Cross with Leeds, Newcastle, Edinburgh and Glasgow. The class was unusual in design, with a raked, sleek cab at the number one end, but a flat-fronted cab at the number two end. This was because they would fit more aerodynamically with the coaching stock, but it was also envisaged that they would haul express parcels and freight traffic overnight. These plans, however, were soon dropped.

All thirty-one members were delivered carrying InterCity Swallow livery, and most received nameplates during this time. They were built to work with the Metro-Cammell-built Mark IV carriages, with both loco and carriages having the same body profiling to help high-speed running. They were also designed to work with a DVT, to avoid uncoupling and run round at terminal stations.

Upon privatisation, the East Coast Main Line would pass to Sea Containers, who ran under the GNER brand. All the locomotives and coaching stock received a new blue livery with a red band along the bodyside.

GNER ran the East Coast line for eleven years, but the franchise changed hands in 2007, with National Express East Coast taking over the route. The Class 91s again changed livery, but with National Express only running the line for two years, not all the locomotives were changed. No. 91111 was the only Class 91 to receive the full National Express livery, with most just having a white band replace the red band.

National Express East Coast ceased to operate in 2009, when the line went back into public ownership, becoming East Coast, who managed to run the franchise successfully for the next six years. During this time, yet another new livery adorned the Class, before the entire fleet was taken over by Virgin Trains East Coast in 2016, resulting in another livery change.

The locomotives themselves have performed faultlessly over the years, and in order to increase availability and reliability the fleet went through a major overhaul from 2001 onwards, known as Project Delta. When the locomotives passed through Doncaster Works for the overhauls, '100' was added to their running numbers to help identify refurbished locomotives.

The only loco that differed was No. 91023, which was renumbered 91132 (out of sequence) as it had been involved in two high-profile accidents, at Hatfield and Great Heck.

No. 91110 currently holds the British high-speed record for a locomotive – 161 mph, which it achieved in 1989 – and as such it carries a special plaque to commemorate the occasion.

Several members of the fleet have carried special commemorative liveries over the years, and some have looked superb, and some less so. They have also carried many different names since they were built; indeed, some have carried two or three different names.

The whole fleet has been based at Bounds Green Depot, North London, ever since their introduction, and they continue to be based there today. The class is scheduled to be replaced by the new IEP Class 800 units from 2018 onwards, and it will be interesting to see what the future holds for these powerful express locomotives.

I hope you enjoy looking through my collection of photographs of an interesting class of locomotive. The photographs are arranged in locomotive order and show how each engine has evolved over time.

No. 91001, 27 October 1989

No. 91001 is seen at London King's Cross carrying InterCity Swallow livery – the livery that all the Class 91 locomotives were delivered carrying. In this shot No. 91001 carries the name *Swallow* and is just over twelve months old. After the first ten locomotives were delivered a gap of around twelve months elapsed before the second batch was delivered.

No. 91001, 12 March 1998

No. 91001 is seen again at London King's Cross, but by this time the InterCity livery has given way to GNER blue livery. The name has been removed and the GNER logo is in white, having yet to be replaced with the gold version.

No. 91101, 7 September 2004

No. 91101 is seen following refurbishment at London King's Cross. The gold GNER logo has replaced the white logo and No. 91101 now carries the name *City of London*. The Class 91 locomotives have been an everyday sight at London King's Cross for nearly thirty years.

No. 91101, 24 March 2009

No. 91101 departs London King's Cross while still carrying GNER blue livery, but it has since gained a white stripe and small National Express branding. Another change is the repositioning of the running number on the cabside, while the *City of London* name has been removed.

No. 91101, 6 August 2009

No. 91101 propels a rake of GNER-liveried Mark IV carriages out of Doncaster, heading for London King's Cross. National Express also applied the running number to the front of the Class 91 locomotives when they took over in 2007.

No. 91101, 4 June 2013

No. 91101 is seen at Leeds station looking superb while carrying a special Flying Scotsman livery. By this time National Express had stopped operating and the route was taken back into public ownership, running under the name East Coast.

No. 91101, 19 September 2016

No. 91101 is seen at London King's Cross carrying the second version of the Flying Scotsman livery. This was based on the Virgin Trains East Coast base livery, as can be seen towards the number two end of the loco. It also now carries a very impressive *Flying Scotsman* nameplate.

No. 91101, 10 June 2017

No. 91101 *Flying Scotsman* runs non-stop through Peterborough with a London King's Cross-bound working. This loco carries this unique livery, and is one of several Class 91s to have carried special liveries over the years.

No. 91002, 20 May 1990

No. 91002 is seen stabled outside Doncaster Works surrounded by Network SouthEast-liveried Class 307 units that were being prepared for service at Neville Hill, Leeds. Note that No. 91002 has lost the front valence below the buffers.

No. 91102, 6 August 2009

No. 91102 is seen departing Doncaster while propelling a service to London King's Cross. The loco carries former GNER livery, but has National Express logos on the white stripe. The loco has also received its full running number on the cab front instead of just the last two numbers.

No. 91102, 4 January 2016

No. 91102 works an express north through Peterborough on the Down fast while carrying Virgin Trains East Coast livery. By this time, No. 91102 had received the name *City of York*.

No. 91102, 15 June 2017

No. 91102 *City of York* is seen departing Newcastle while heading for Edinburgh Waverley with a Virgin Trains East Coast working. This loco has also carried the name *Durham Cathedral* during its career.

No. 91003, 20 October 1990

No. 91003 is seen at London King's Cross in as-delivered condition. The class has only ever worked on the East Coast Main Line coupled to a rake of Metro-Cammell-built Mark IV carriages. This loco visited Hamburg in Germany during 1988 along with Nos 89001, 90008 and 150263 as part of the International Transport and Traffic Exhibition.

No. 91103, 23 August 2007

No. 91103 is seen powering north through Doncaster with a GNER working. The loco and stock still carry full GNER livery, and No. 91103 also carries the name *County of Lincolnshire*. The GNER names were just transfers in the middle of the bodyside.

No. 91103, 27 November 2008

No. 91103 stands at London King's Cross, waiting to depart north. By this time No. 91103 had lost its *County of Lincolnshire* name, and GNER had also lost the running of the East Coast Main Line to National Express.

No. 91103, 4 June 2013

No. 91103 is seen standing at York with a northbound working. In 2009 the East Coast franchise had been taken back in house by the Department for Transport and was operated under the East Coast banner, in whose livery No. 91103 is seen.

No. 91103, 25 February 2017

No. 91103 is seen passing by Alexandra Palace while propelling a Virgin Trains East Coast working through to London King's Cross. The train is approximately ten minutes from its destination.

No. 91103, 26 January 2018

No. 91103 is seen departing Doncaster, heading south. The Power Signal Box can be seen in the background. The signal box was opened in 1981 and most of the signaling will transfer to York in 2020, with the box due to fully close in 2025. This loco has carried the named *County of Lincolnshire* and *The Scotsman* during its career.

No. 91004, 24 October 1996

No. 91004 is seen arriving at Leeds with a terminating service from London King's Cross. This loco still carries full InterCity Swallow livery and the name *The Red Arrows*, despite working for GNER at the time.

No. 91104, 6 August 2009

No. 91104 departs from Doncaster with a southbound National Express East Coast working. The loco still carries GNER blue livery, but with the addition of a white stripe carrying National Express logos. This loco has carried the names *The Red Arrows* and *Grantham* during its career.

No. 91104, 12 March 2015

No. 91104 stands at London King's Cross having arrived with a terminating Virgin Trains East Coast working. The loco carries East Coast base livery, but has had Virgin Trains vinyls added. Note the Mark IV carriages still carrying East Coast website details.

No. 91104, 15 June 2017

No. 91104 stands in the sun at Newcastle having arrived with a terminating Virgin Trains East Coast working from London King's Cross. The loco carries full Virgin Trains livery, and has matching Mark IV carriages.

No. 91005, 20 May 1990

No. 91005 slows for the station call at Doncaster with a northbound InterCity East Coast working. This was taken at the time when a number of the class had the front valence removed from under the buffers, leaving a very untidy appearance.

No. 91005, 29 June 1991

No. 91005 is seen a long way from the East Coast while on display at Bristol's St Philip's Marsh open day. The loco was open for cab visits, and by this time the front valence had been reattached under the buffers.

No. 91105, 6 August 2009

No. 91105 is seen arriving at Doncaster with a northbound National Express East Coast working. During its career, No. 91105 has carried the names *County Durham* and *Royal Air Force Regiment*. No. 91105 is seen carrying the interim livery of GNER blue, but with the National Express white stripe added.

No. 91105, 16 March 2016

No. 91105 is seen powering northwards through Peterborough at the head of a Virgin Trains East Coast working. All thirty-one members of the class are still in use on East Coast express workings, working for Virgin Trains.

No. 91105, 19 September 2016.

No. 91105 is seen running at speed through Alexandra Palace while heading north. The whole class was refurbished at Doncaster Works from 2000 onwards under Project Delta, which resulted in them having '100' added to their running numbers.

No. 91105, 14 August 2017

No. 91105 stands at London King's Cross, waiting to depart north. By this time, it had received new LED headlights to improve visibility for track workers. The red Virgin Trains livery certainly brightens up the appearance of the class.

No. 91006, 29 October 1995

No. 91006 is seen stabled at Polmadie Depot, Glasgow, waiting to enter service for the day. This loco later carried the name *East Lothian* when in use with GNER. Another rake of Mark IV carriages can be seen to the left.

No. 91106, 1 August 2013

No. 91106 is seen at London King's Cross having arrived with a terminating East Coast working. East Coast operated the franchise for just over five years from 2009, and was run by the Department for Transport before the franchise was re-let and won by the Stagecoach Group, trading as Virgin Trains East Coast.

No. 91106, 12 March 2015

No. 91106 is seen waiting to depart northwards from London King's Cross while carrying former East Coast livery, but with Virgin Trains branding applied. Today, the whole fleet carries full Virgin Trains East Coast livery, except for the handful of commemorative-liveried examples.

No. 91106, 4 January 2016

No. 91106 speeds north through Peterborough at the head of a Virgin Trains East Coast working. The loco is still carrying former East Coast livery but with Virgin Trains branding, while the rake of Mark IV carriages carries full Virgin Trains livery.

No. 91106, 26 January 2018

No. 91106 arrives at Doncaster with the winter sunshine glinting off the bodywork. Like the rest of the fleet this loco, except for the commemorative-liveried examples, carries Virgin Trains East Coast livery.

No. 91007, 20 May 1990

No. 91007 is seen stabled in one of the bay platforms at Doncaster. This view shows the loco from the number two, or 'blunt' end. It was originally envisaged that the locos would work overnight parcels and freight traffic using this end, but the idea was quickly dropped and the locomotives were used exclusively on passenger workings instead.

No. 91107, 20 March 2003

No. 91107 *Newark on Trent* is seen carrying GNER blue livery while heading north at Doncaster. This was one of the first Class 91s to pass through Doncaster for refurbishment under Project Delta, which improved reliability for the class.

No. 91107, 7 September 2004

No. 91107 is seen at London King's Cross carrying GNER blue livery, waiting to depart north. This loco carries the name *Newark on Trent*, but has also carried the names *Ian Allan* and *Skyfall 007*.

No. 91107, 6 August 2009

No. 91107 is seen slowing for the station call at Doncaster. By this time the East Coast franchise had been taken over by National Express, with most of the class receiving white stripes covering over the GNER orange stripe, and also covering up the names in the process.

No. 91107, 22 March 2013

No. 91107 stands at London King's Cross, having arrived with a terminating service. The loco is seen carrying advertising livery for the James Bond film *Skyfall*, complete with a matching rake of Mark IV carriages. The loco was still officially known as No. 91107, but the number had been changed to No. 91007, and it also received the vinyl nameplate *Skyfall 007*, which was carried on the front corner.

No. 91107, 29 June 2015

No. 91107 is seen standing in the summer sunshine at London King's Cross. The loco had lost its advertising livery by this time but, as can be seen, it had received a cast *Skyfall 007* nameplate. The loco carries Virgin Trains East Coast livery, but the carriages still retain East Coast livery.

No. 91107, 16 March 2016

No. 91107 *Skyfall 007* is seen making a station call at Peterborough while heading for London King's Cross. Peterborough was always a good place to see these locomotives in action, as they both passed straight through at speed and also made station calls.

No. 91008, 31 August 1996

No. 91008 is seen at Edinburgh Waverley still carrying full InterCity Swallow livery, despite having been in GNER ownership for the previous four months. The loco is seen from the number two end, and also carries the name *Thomas Cook*.

No. 91008, 30 June 1999

No. 91008 is seen at London King's Cross carrying GNER livery. Some of the first GNER repaints received white logos, but all soon changed to the gold ones, as seen here. No. 91008 is seen devoid of any name.

No. 91108, 4 June 2013

No. 91108 is seen underneath the magnificent arch roof at York while propelling an East Coast service to London King's Cross. The loco carries full East Coast livery. No. 91108 has carried the names *City of Leeds* and *Thomas Cook* during its career.

No. 91108, 15 June 2017

No. 91108 departs from Leeds while propelling a Virgin Trains East Coast working through to London King's Cross. The service to Leeds runs half-hourly, and all services terminate before heading back south.

No. 91009, 3 August 1990

No. 91009 is seen arriving at London King's Cross, with its blunt end leading, with a rake of charter stock Mark I carriages as an empty coaching stock move. These carriages always stood out with their white roofs.

No. 91009, 26 June 1993

No. 91009 arrives at Doncaster complete with *Saint Nicholas* nameplate. Note the missing cover from the loco front – a feature that was not a regular appearance.

No. 91009, 26 October 1996

No. 91009 arrives at Leeds with a terminating service from London King's Cross. This loco was operated by GNER at the time, but still retained full InterCity Swallow livery, complete with large cast *Saint Nicholas* nameplates.

No. 91009, 23 October 1998

No. 91009 is seen being shunted around Doncaster by Class 08 No. 08682. The loco has recently been inside the works and has received a new set of bogies. By this time it carries the name *The Samaritans*.

No. 91109, 7 September 2004

No. 91109 *The Samaritans* is seen stabled at London King's Cross while on standby duty. The loco is seen from the number two, or blunt end, and is seen along with classmate No. 91121. Of note is the Class 373 Eurostar unit alongside, which was on hire to GNER at the time.

No. 91109, 15 October 2008

No. 91109 is seen arriving at Glasgow Central, crossing over the River Clyde. By this time the loco was operated by National Express and had received the white stripe to cover the GNER logos. The loco still carries its *The Samaritans* name, but it is carried in very small letters halfway along the white stripe.

No. 91109, 4 June 2013

No. 91109 stands in one of the bay platforms at York having arrived from London King's Cross. The loco carries full East Coast livery and by this time had been renamed *Sir Bobby Robson* after the former England football player and manager, who passed away in 2009.

No. 91109, 16 March 2016

No. 91109 powers northwards through Peterborough while carrying Virgin Trains East Coast livery. The loco still carries its *Sir Bobby Robson* nameplates in this view.

No. 91010, 8 July 2000

No. 91010 is seen arriving at Edinburgh Waverley while propelling a rake of GNER-liveried Mark IV carriages. This was the last loco of the initial order for Class 91 locomotives, with the delivery of the second batch starting nearly twelve months after No. 91010.

No. 91110, 27 November 2008

No. 91110 stands at London King's Cross carrying former GNER blue livery, but with National Express logos. The loco also carries a very small *David Livingstone* name halfway along the white stripe. No. 91110 carries a special plaque to commemorate its British locomotive speed record of 161 mph.

No. 91110, 12 June 2012

No. 91110 *Battle of Britain Memorial Flight Spitfire Hurricane Lancaster Dakota* departs London King's Cross carrying its very special RAF-dedicated livery. This view shows the speed record plaque underneath the cab window.

No. 91110, 19 September 2016

No. 91110 *Battle of Britain Memorial Flight Spitfire Hurricane Lancaster Dakota* is seen from the opposite side to the previous photograph, showing the different vinyl used on this side of the loco. No. 91110 has also carried the name *Northern Rock* during its career.

No. 91110, 19 September 2016

The very impressive nameplate as fitted to No. 91110 *Battle of Britain Memorial Flight Spitfire Hurricane Lancaster Dakota*. This loco carries a special Battle of Britain Memorial Flight vinyl.

No. 91110, 15 June 2017

No. 91110 departs from Darlington station while propelling a rake of Virgin Trains-liveried Mark IV carriages towards London King's Cross. This loco carries the hugely impressive *Battle of Britain Memorial Flight Spitfire Hurricane Lancaster Dakota* nameplate.

No. 91011, 25 October 1996

No. 91011 is seen arriving at Doncaster carrying InterCity Swallow livery. This loco carries the name *Terence Cuneo* and also carried a small mouse on its bodyside in commemoration of its namesake. Terence Cuneo was a world-renowned artist, made famous for his railway paintings, and there was a mouse hidden away in almost every one of his paintings.

No. 91011, 18 August 1999

No. 91011 arrives at Leeds with a GNER working from London King's Cross. Of note is the West Yorkshire Metro-liveried Class 308 unit in the background, which was used around Yorkshire until the new Class 333 units arrived for service.

No. 91111, 2 August 2007

No. 91111 is seen slowing for the station call at Peterborough while heading northwards with a GNER working. By this time the loco had been reunited with its *Terence Cuneo* name, despite it now being just a transfer on the bodyside.

No. 91111, 24 March 2009

No. 91111 stands at London King's Cross having arrived with a terminating service. This loco carries full National Express East Coast livery, and as the franchise was only held for a short time by National Express, this was the only Class 91 to carry the full livery.

No. 91111, 6 August 2009

No. 91111 departs Doncaster while propelling a rake of Mark IV carriages towards London King's Cross. This was the only Class 91 to carry full National Express white and silver livery, and in this livery it never carried a name.

No. 91111, 16 March 2016

No. 91111 is seen working non-stop through Peterborough while heading for London King's Cross. This loco was chosen in 2014 to receive a special First World War commemorative vinyl, and also received the name *For The Fallen* at the same time.

No. 91012, 30 December 1996

No. 91012 is seen arriving at Doncaster carrying recently applied GNER blue livery. This loco has carried the name *County of Cambridgeshire* during its career, but at the time of the photograph it was nameless.

No. 91112, 18 October 2004

No. 91112 *County of Cambridgeshire* is seen having arrived at London King's Cross. The loco carries full GNER livery, complete with gold logos, and matching Mark IV carriages.

No. 91112, 16 March 2016

No. 91112 is seen making the station call at Peterborough while propelling a Virgin Trains East Coast working through to London King's Cross. This view shows the pleasing Virgin Trains livery off well.

No. 91112, 25 March 2016

No. 91112 is seen having arrived at London King's Cross with a terminating service. The Class 91 Electra locomotives are due to be replaced on the East Coast route by new Class 800 Hitachi-built units, with Virgin Trains retaining just a handful of sets.

No. 91013, 6 May 1990

No. 91013 is seen as one of the stars of the show at Bescot open day 1990. This loco was brand new at the time, and this is one of the only times I've seen a member of the class in the West Midlands.

No. 91013, 17 May 1997

No. 91013 is seen at London King's Cross having propelled a GNER working into the station. The loco is most unusually facing south, meaning that the blunt end will be leading when it departs from King's Cross. It is very unusual to see a Class 91 facing south while working.

No. 91113, 6 August 2009

No. 91113 is seen departing Doncaster while propelling a National Express East Coast working through to London King's Cross. This loco has carried the names *County of North Yorkshire* and *Sir Michael Faraday* during its career.

No. 91113, 12 March 2015

No. 91113 is seen at London King's Cross, waiting to depart back north. This loco is seen carrying the former East Coast base livery, but with new Virgin Trains logos applied over the top.

No. 91113, 29 June 2015

No. 91113 powers southbound through Alexandra Palace while propelling a Virgin Trains East Coast working to London King's Cross. The loco still retains its East Coast livery, but with Virgin Trains logos added. The carriages still retained their East Coast livery and logos.

No. 91014, 4 April 1995

No. 91014 *Northern Electric* is seen waiting to depart from London King's Cross alongside classmate No. 91027 *Great North Run*, which had only been named five days previously. At this time the East Coast route was still operated by the InterCity sector.

No. 91114, 23 August 2007

No. 91114 is seen slowing for the station call at Doncaster while carrying full GNER blue livery. By this time the loco had also changed names, and now carried the name *St Mungo Cathedral*.

No. 91114, 26 November 2007

No. 91114 *St Mungo Cathedral* is seen at London King's Cross carrying a strange combination of liveries. The loco still retains full GNER blue livery, complete with gold logos, but with the East Coast Main Line to be taken over by National Express two weeks later, they had added the running number to the front of the loco and the cabside, but had yet to add the white stripe similar to the carriages behind.

No. 91114, 27 November 2008

No. 91114 is seen twelve months after the previous photograph, and by this time the white stripe had been added, the GNER logos removed and the *St Mungo Cathedral* name had been covered over by the white stripe, though it was still carried in very small letters halfway along the white stripe.

No. 91114, 19 March 2013

No. 91114 is seen resting at London King's Cross while carrying a combination of three different operators' liveries! The loco carries former GNER blue livery, but also has a white stripe that was applied by National Express, though their logos have been removed with East Coast logos applied instead.

No. 91114, 10 March 2015

No. 91114 is seen departing Leeds while propelling a Virgin Trains East Coast working to London King's Cross. This loco carries the name *Durham Cathedral* and also has some minor livery differences, with the purple stripe extending right round the front to the yellow, and it also carries some small railway decals above the purple stripe, underneath the name.

No. 91114, 4 January 2016

No. 91114 *Durham Cathedral* is seen making a station call at Peterborough. This loco also carries livery differences, carrying Virgin Train East Coast livery with the white cathedral on the bodyside, and also the triangular patterns on the grey part of the body.

No. 91114, 16 March 2016

No. 91114 is seen propelling a Virgin Trains East Coast working into Peterborough. This view shows the second duplex pantograph as uniquely fitted to this Class 91. The loco also carries 'The Very Reverend Michael Sadgrove Dean of Durham 2003–2013' decals underneath the cab window, as well as the name *Durham Cathedral*.

No. 91114, 26 January 2018

No. 91114 *Durham Cathedral* is seen at Doncaster, having been rescued by the East Coast Thunderbird Class 67 No. 67010, and is being hauled south for attention. Note the lowered pantograph and the tail lamp in place.

No. 91015, 17 August 1991

No. 91015 stands at London King's Cross while carrying full InterCity Swallow livery. This loco had only been in service for just over a year and would go on to receive the name *Holyrood*.

No. 91015, 1 March 1997

No. 91015 is seen at London King's Cross having recently being outshopped from overhaul, including a repaint into GNER blue livery. Of note are the Mark IV carriages, and the full InterCity 225 set alongside, which still retain their InterCity liveries.

No. 91115, 29 August 2006

No. 91115 is seen arriving at Leeds with a GNER working from London King's Cross. By this time the locomotive had been through the Project Delta refurbishment programme at Doncaster, and carried the name *Holyrood*.

No. 91115, 26 November 2007

No. 91115 *Holyrood* rests at London King's Cross while carrying GNER blue livery. National Express were to take over the running of the East Coast route within two weeks of this photograph, and the loco had already received the white running number on the cabside.

No. 91115, 24 March 2009

No. 91115 slowly arrives at London King's Cross with a service from the north. By this time the loco had received the full intermediate National Express livery of former GNER blue, but with the full white stripe and National Express logos. Unlike other members of the class, No. 91115 didn't retain its *Holyrood* name in very small letters on the white stripe.

No. 91115, 6 August 2009

No. 91115 is seen making a station call at Doncaster's Platform 1 with a National Express East Coast working to London King's Cross. At this time the locomotive was approaching twenty years of service on the East Coast.

No. 91115, 16 July 2013

No. 91115 is seen arriving at Leeds while carrying full East Coast livery. By this time the loco had received the name *Blaydon Races* and the East Coast route was back in public ownership, before being awarded to Stagecoach Rail, trading as Virgin Trains East Coast.

No. 91115, 12 March 2015

No. 91115 *Blaydon Races* is seen waiting to depart from London King's Cross. The loco still retains East Coast livery, despite Stagecoach Rail having taken over the route two weeks previously. As with all other members of the class, No. 91115 would go on to receive Virgin Trains East Coast livery.

No. 91016, 26 October 1996

No. 91016 is seen arriving at Leeds with a GNER working from London King's Cross. GNER had taken over operating the East Coast route in April 1996. The Class 91 locomotives took a lot of inspiration from the APT, and were introduced following the electrification of the whole East Coast route.

No. 91116, 6 August 2009

No. 91116 is seen slowing for the station call at Doncaster with a northbound National Express East Coast working. This loco has only ever carried the one name during its career, *Strathclyde*.

No. 91116, 16 July 2013

No. 91116 is seen rounding the curve into Leeds station with a terminating East Coast working from London King's Cross. All Class 91 locomotives received the East Coast livery during the five years that the route was run back in public ownership.

No. 91116, 4 January 2016

No. 91116 is seen making a station call at Peterborough while propelling a Virgin Trains East Coast working to London King's Cross. This locomotive, like the majority of the class, has led a very uneventful life, but their service on the East Coast route over the years has been invaluable.

No. 91017, 30 December 1996

No. 91017 is seen arriving at Doncaster while carrying recently applied GNER blue livery. The rake of Mark IV carriages coupled behind still retains its InterCity livery.

No. 91117, 24 March 2009

No. 91117 awaits departure time at London King's Cross with a National Express East Coast working north. This loco has carried the names *Cancer Research UK* and *Commonwealth Institute* during its career, and now carries the name *West Riding Limited*.

No. 91117, 16 March 2016

No. 91117 *West Riding Limited* slows for the station call at Peterborough while carrying Virgin Trains East Coast livery. All of the class now carry these colours, apart from the special commemorative-liveried examples.

No. 91018, 4 April 1995

No. 91018 is seen having arrived at London King's Cross. The loco carries the name *Robert Louis Stevenson*, and there is no doubt that the class looked good in InterCity Swallow livery. No. 91018 was named after the famous Scottish novelist, whose works include *Kidnapped* and *Treasure Island*.

No. 91118, 11 September 2005

No. 91118 is seen sat on a low loader during the Crewe Works open day in 2005. Crewe Works always put on a good show during their open days, and No. 91118 is returning to where it was built fifteen years previously. By this time the loco had changed its name to *Bradford Film Festival*.

No. 91118, 10 March 2015

No. 91118 is seen arriving at Leeds carrying East Coast livery. By this time all the locos had received flush fronts, with the two opening panels beneath the windscreens having been plated over.

No. 91118, 12 March 2015

No. 91118 arrives at London King's Cross on the rear of an East Coast working. This view not only shows the impressive length of these locos; the cardan shafts can also be clearly seen, leading from the bogie-mounted gearbox to the traction motors mounted on the body.

No. 91118, 26 January 2018

No. 91118 departs Doncaster while propelling a Virgin Trains East Coast working to London King's Cross. Of note is the fact the loco is missing the front skirt around the couplings.

No. 91019, 12 July 1992

No. 91019 is seen inside Doncaster Works during the open day of 1992. The loco is seen undergoing collision repairs and had only been in service for two years at the time. The loco carries *Scottish Enterprise* nameplates.

No. 91019, 24 October 1996

No. 91019 is seen having arrived at Leeds with a terminating GNER working. This was one of the first class members to receive the GNER blue livery, and note how the orange stripe doesn't match up correctly with the stripe on the attached Mark IV carriage. The loco retained its *Scottish Enterprise* name.

No. 91119, 6 August 2009

No. 91119 arrives at Doncaster with a National Express East Coast working to the north. By this time the loco had lost its *Scottish Enterprise* name, and had also carried the name *County of Tyne and Wear*, but currently carries the name *Bounds Green InterCity Depot*.

No. 91119, 1 August 2013

No. 91119 is seen having arrived at London King's Cross. This loco is seen carrying parts of liveries from three different operators of the East Coast – the plain blue being GNER and the white stripe being National Express East Coast – but their logos have been replaced with East Coast logos.

No. 91119, 26 January 2018

No. 91119 is seen departing Doncaster with a service towards London King's Cross. This loco is seen carrying the name *Bounds Green InterCity Depot*, named after the whole fleet's home depot in North London. Bounds Green has maintained the fleet since its introduction.

No. 91020, 24 October 1996

No. 91020, carrying InterCity Swallow livery, arrives at Leeds with a terminating service. GNER had taken over operation of the route by this time, but they were slow to apply their livery and logos. No. 91020 later carried the name *Royal Armouries*.

No. 91120, 16 September 2015

No. 91120 is seen having arrived at Edinburgh Waverley. The loco carries former East Coast livery, but with large Virgin Trains branding applied. By this time No. 91120 had lost its *Royal Armouries* name. The Royal Armouries is the United Kingdom's National Museum of Arms and Armour and is based in Leeds.

No. 91120, 4 January 2016

No. 91120 slows for the station call at Peterborough with a northbound working. This is one of quite a few members of the class that didn't carry a nameplate at this time, although every loco has carried a name at some point over their careers.

No. 91021, 27 March 1991

No. 91021 is seen with a similar working to the previous photograph, but taken twenty-five years previously. These two shots show how the class has been the mainstay of electrically hauled East Coast workings for the past twenty-five years.

No. 91121, 7 September 2004

No. 91121 stands in the loco stabling sidings at London King's Cross while on standby duty, along with classmate No. 91109. It was unusual to get two standby Class 91s stabled. No. 91121 carries the name *Archbishop Thomas Cranmer*.

No. 91121, 2 August 2007

No. 91121 *Archbishop Thomas Cranmer* slows for the station call at Peterborough carrying full GNER livery. GNER only had another four months running the East Coast ahead of it, before National Express took over. *Archbishop Thomas Cranmer* was the leader of the English Reformation, and was also the Archbishop of Canterbury during Tudor times.

No. 91121, 27 November 2008

No. 91121 is seen at London King's Cross, waiting to depart north. By this time the East Coast had been taken over by National Express, and No. 91121 carries the interim livery of GNER blue but with a white stripe covering the orange. The very small name *Archbishop Thomas Cranmer* can just be seen halfway along the white stripe.

No. 91121, 22 March 2013

No. 91121 arrives at London King's Cross with a terminating service. The loco has by this time received East Coast logos on top of the former National Express logos as well as a repainted yellow front end, removing the last two running numbers in the process. Alongside is Class 43 No. 43277 carrying full East Coast livery.

No. 91121, 25 October 2017

No. 91121 is seen at Newcastle having arrived with a terminating Virgin Trains East Coast working, and is waiting to head back towards London King's Cross. Virgin Trains will cease to run the franchise in 2020, with the possibility of yet another different operator working the route.

No. 91121, 26 January 2018

No. 91121 is seen arriving at Doncaster while propelling a Virgin Trains East Coast working northwards. The reverse working is quite rare on this route, as the loco is normally at the country end of the formation.

No. 91022, 4 April 1995

No. 91022 is seen waiting to depart from London King's Cross while carrying InterCity Swallow livery. By this time the loco had been named *Robert Adley*, one of three names this loco would carry in its career, the others being *Tam the Gun* and *Double Trigger*.

No. 91022, 6 April 1997

No. 91022 is seen at York carrying recently applied GNER blue livery. This was one of the locos that carried the short-lived white GNER logos, which were all changed to the normal gold.

No. 91122, 23 August 2007

No. 91122 *Tam the Gun* departs from Doncaster. 'Tam the Gun' was the nickname given to Staff Sergeant Thomas McKay MBE, who was responsible for the daily one o'clock firing of the gun at Edinburgh Castle before he passed away in 2005.

No. 91122, 27 November 2008

No. 91122 is seen at London King's Cross carrying the interim National Express East Coast livery. The full National Express livery was only carried by one Class 91, No. 91111. No. 91122 carries a very small *Tam the Gun* name halfway along the white stripe.

No. 91122, 6 August 2009

No. 91122 travels northbound through Doncaster with a non-stop working. The loco and stock carry the matching interim National Express East Coast livery.

No. 91122, 15 June 2017

No. 91122 arrives at Darlington underneath the very impressive train shed still *in situ* there. By this time the loco has received Virgin Trains East Coast livery and is seen without a name.

No. 91023, 7 September 1991

No. 91023 is seen departing Leeds with an InterCity working to London King's Cross. This had only been in service for twelve months, but is seen during the period when some members of the class had their front valences removed.

No. 91023, 30 December 1996

No. 91023 is seen having arrived at Doncaster with evidence of snow on the buffers and rubbing plate. This loco would go onto win notoriety when it was involved in two fatal incidents in 2000 and 2001. This loco has only ever carried the one name, *City of Durham*.

No. 91023, 18 August 1997

No. 91023 waits to depart northwards from London King's Cross. By this time the loco had received GNER blue livery, but still retained the white logos. This loco was involved in the Hatfield disaster of 2000, which resulted in the loss of four lives, and the more serious Great Heck collision of 2001, which claimed ten lives, including four members of railway staff.

No. 91023, 27 March 1998

No. 91023 leads an impressive line-up at London King's Cross of five Class 91 locomotives and a sole Class 89, No. 89001. The Class 89 was a prototype loco built at Crewe Works in the mid-1980s and was used on the East Coast route alongside the Class 91 locomotives.

No. 91132, 12 June 2012

No. 91132 is seen at London King's Cross carrying full East Coast livery. Following No. 91023's involvement in the two fatal incidents, it was decided to alter the running number upon refurbishment, and instead of emerging as No. 91123, the loco was renumbered No. 91132 out of superstition.

No. 91132, 16 March 2016

No. 91132 departs Peterborough with a southbound Virgin Trains East Coast working. Since this view, the loco has received some mental health awareness vinyls.

No. 91024, 12 October 1994

No. 91024 is seen having arrived at Edinburgh Waverley. This loco was later named *Reverend W. Awdry*, and this is the only plate this loco has ever carried. Reverend W. Awdry was most famous for his literary work, responsible for creating the Thomas the Tank Engine series of books.

No. 91124, 12 March 2015

No. 91124 is seen at London King's Cross, waiting to depart northwards. By this time No. 91124 had been repainted into Virgin Trains East Coast livery; meanwhile, classmate No. 91131 alongside still carries former East Coast livery.

No. 91124, 16 March 2016

No. 91124 arrives at Peterborough carrying Virgin Trains East Coast livery, with a complete matching rake of Mark IV carriages behind. Over 300 Mark IV carriages were built by Metro-Cammell in Birmingham, all of which were refurbished, except for twelve which were scrapped following serious incidents.

No. 91124, 15 June 2017

No. 91124 is seen in the summer sun at Newcastle while departing northwards towards Edinburgh Waverley. The Class 91 locos are due to be mostly replaced by Hitachi-built Class 800 units in the future.

No. 91025, 31 August 1996

No. 91025 is seen stabled at Heaton Depot, Newcastle, carrying InterCity Swallow livery. This view shows the different styles of cabs used at either end of these powerful locomotives. No. 91025 carries the name *BBC Radio 1 FM*.

No. 91125, 29 August 2006

No. 91125 is seen arriving at Platform 8, Doncaster, with a northbound GNER working. The loco is seen carrying the name *Berwick-upon-Tweed*, the names being applied as transfers during the GNER period.

No. 91125, 2 August 2007

No. 91125 *Berwick-upon-Tweed* arrives at Peterborough from the south. Not all of the East Coast services made station calls at Peterborough, with a number passing through on the fast lines in the centre of the station.

No. 91125, 16 September 2015

No. 91125 is seen awaiting departure time at Edinburgh Waverley with a Virgin Trains East Coast working to London King's Cross. Note that the loco still retains former East Coast livery, but with Virgin Trains logos applied, whereas the carriages have already received the full Virgin Trains livery.

No. 91125, 16 March 2016

No. 91125 arrives at Peterborough while at the head of a Virgin Trains East Coast working. Note the LED headlights that have now been fitted to the whole class. This loco has also carried a special Sky One advertising livery in connection with the channel airing a documentary series about the East Coast operator.

No. 91125, 15 June 2017

No. 91125 departs from Darlington with a southbound working. The loco seems to only have one working taillight, though both are in fact working, the second light flickering in and out of use. Darlington still retains its very impressive train shed, as can be seen.

No. 91026, 1 March 1997

No. 91026 is seen having arrived at London King's Cross with a terminating service. This loco carries the name *Voice of the North*, which can be seen adjacent to the InterCity logo. Some of the plates at this time were cast, like this one; others were made of cheaper aluminium.

No. 91026, 6 April 1997

No. 91026 *Voice of the North* arrives at York while propelling its InterCity service towards London King's Cross. This view shows the number two cab flush with the first carriage. The adjacent carriage doesn't have a gangway connection fitted at the end next to the loco, the end instead being plated over.

No. 91026, 21 June 1999

No. 91026 is seen at Doncaster, unusually with its number one cab coupled to its rake of Mark IV carriages. It was very unusual to see the loco coupled in this way, as it would either have to use a turntable or be turned on a triangle to get back facing the right way.

No. 91126, 9 February 2004

No. 91126 *York Minster* is seen being shunted around Doncaster by the resident Class 08 locomotive. Before it was closed and demolished, Doncaster Works was always responsible for the major overhauls to the Class 91 fleet. This view shows the locomotive from its flush number two cab end.

No. 91126, 18 October 2004

No. 91126 is seen back in traffic following its visit to Doncaster earlier in the year. The loco carries the name *York Minster*, but has also carried the names *Voice of the North* and *Darlington Hippodrome* during its career.

No. 91126, 16 March 2016

No. 91126 powers northwards on the Down fast through Peterborough. Since this shot was taken, No. 91126 has been named *Darlington Hippodrome*.

No. 91027, 18 August 1995

No. 91027 is seen at London King's Cross, complete with 'not to be moved' board attached. This was added as the Mark IV carriages are serviced while at King's Cross, with all water being replenished. No. 91027 carries the name *Great North Run*.

No. 91027, 18 August 1999

No. 91027 is seen departing from Leeds carrying GNER blue livery. This is another example of the stock being in reverse formation, as the loco should be at the other end of the working. Note the slam-door Class 308 unit behind; these were used until the Class 333 units entered service.

No. 91127, 1 April 2003

No. 91127 is seen at London King's Cross, having arrived with a terminating service. This was the first Class 91 to go through the Project Delta refurbishment at Doncaster, which resulted in the class being renumbered. No. 91127 carries the name *Edinburgh Castle*.

No. 91127, 19 March 2013

No. 91127 is seen at London King's Cross carrying East Coast livery. This loco had arrived as an empty coaching stock move from Bounds Green. No. 91127 is seen without a name, but it has carried the names *Great North Run* and *Edinburgh Castle* during its career.

No. 91127, 13 June 2013

No. 91127 is seen at London King's Cross carrying East Coast livery. East Coast operated the route for just over five years before handing over to Virgin Trains East Coast in February 2015.

No. 91028, 6 April 1997

No. 91028 is seen at the north end of Leeds station having arrived from London King's Cross. At this time the loco carried the name *Guide Dog*, and still looked very respectable in its InterCity Swallow livery.

No. 91028, 4 May 1997

No. 91028 is seen departing Darlington while propelling a GNER working to London King's Cross. This shot was taken just four weeks after the previous photograph, and during that month the loco had been repainted into GNER blue with white logos, losing its *Guide Dog* name.

No. 91128, 4 June 2013

No. 91128 is seen in the impressive station surroundings at York. The loco carries East Coast livery, complete with a matching rake of Mark IV carriages.

No. 91128, 13 June 2013

No. 91128 rests at London King's Cross having arrived from the north. This loco has carried three different names during its career: *Guide Dog*, *Peterborough Cathedral* and *InterCity 50*.

No. 91128, 16 July 2013

No. 91128 is seen arriving at Leeds with a terminating East Coast working from London King's Cross. Leeds has gone through some major rebuilding over the years, with No. 91128 arriving where the former parcels bays were situated.

No. 91128, 4 January 2016

No. 91128 is seen arriving at Peterborough with a Virgin Trains East Coast working. This loco was chosen to be re-vinyled during December 2015 and carries a special Christmas livery. Mark IV DVT No. 82209 carried a similar livery.

No. 91128, 4 January 2016

No. 91128 is seen from the number two cab end, showing its special Christmas Claus 91 livery. Virgin Trains ran a couple of Christmas-liveried Class 390 units on the West Coast route for a couple of festive periods, but this was the only Class 91 so treated, and it soon reverted to normal Virgin Trains East Coast livery.

No. 91128, 15 June 2017

No. 91128 *InterCity 50* is seen having arrived at Newcastle with a terminating Virgin Trains East Coast working. The loco then departed north, running via the old Gateshead Depot, before returning to this very spot about fifteen minutes later, arriving from the south.

No. 91128 and No. 91102, 15 June 2017

No. 91128 *InterCity 50* is seen at Newcastle alongside classmate No. 91102 *City of York*. Both locomotives represent the current face of Virgin Trains East Coast, but what does the future hold for the class once the Class 800 units are in service?

No. 91029, 1 March 1997

No. 91029 is seen waiting to depart from London King's Cross while carrying InterCity Swallow livery and named *Queen Elizabeth II*, which is the only name the loco has ever carried.

No. 91029, 18 August 1999

No. 91029 is seen departing Leeds on the back of a GNER working to London King's Cross. By this time the loco had been repainted into GNER blue livery, but it is already starting to look a little scruffy. It has also lost its *Queen Elizabeth II* name.

No. 91129, 20 January 2009

No. 91129 arrives at London King's Cross with a terminating service. This photograph was taken when National Express had taken over the running of the East Coast franchise from GNER.

No. 91129, 6 August 2009

No. 91129 is seen making a station call at Doncaster. National Express was very slow when it came to repainting its Class 91 fleet, with only No. 91111 carrying the full livery while the rest appeared like No. 91129.

No. 91129, 12 June 2012

No. 91129 is seen in the newest platform at London King's Cross, Platform 0. This new platform was added following the demolition of the buildings that were previously situated where No. 91129 can be seen.

No. 91129, 22 August 2016

No. 91129 arrives at Leeds with a Virgin Trains East Coast working from London King's Cross. Note that the loco has yet to receive its LED headlights, which have been fitted to the class to improve visibility.

No. 91129, 25 February 2017

No. 91129 stands at London King's Cross waiting to depart with the 09.30 Virgin Trains East Coast service to Edinburgh Waverley. This journey is scheduled to take just under four hours and forty-five minutes.

No. 91129, 14 August 2017

No. 91129 stands ready to depart northwards from London King's Cross. By this time the loco has had new LED headlights fitted, and it also carries a British Rail style BN Bounds Green Depot sticker underneath the running number.

No. 91030, 6 March 1995

No. 91030 *Palace of Holyroodhouse* is seen at London King's Cross. The nameplate carried on this loco is one of the aluminium examples, which don't stand out as well as the cast nameplates. Note how the InterCity Swallow-liveried examples also carried a small Swallow on the warning horn cover.

No. 91030 and No. 91013, 17 May 1997

No. 91030 and No. 91013 are seen side-by-side at London King's Cross. This view shows the two different styles of cab off nicely, with the familiar streamlined end on No. 91030 on the left contrasting with the flush cab front on No. 91013 on the right. Both locomotives carry GNER blue livery.

No. 91030, 6 April 1998

No. 91030 passes through Thirsk while propelling a GNER working towards London King's Cross. This view shows the white GNER logos that were applied for a short time to some members of the class, before all were replaced with the familiar gold logos. It also shows the cast GNER crest that was carried by the Mark IV carriages.

No. 91130, 13 August 2004

No. 91130 *City of Newcastle* is seen departing from Doncaster while heading for London King's Cross. The large black building is Doncaster Power Signal Box. Doncaster was, and still is, a great place to see the Class 91s, with most of the class passing through during the day.

No. 91130, 6 August 2009

No. 91130 is seen powering northwards through the centre road at Doncaster. In this view the loco is nameless, but before this shot the loco had carried the names *Palace of Holyroodhouse* and *City of Newcastle*.

No. 91130, 10 June 2017

No. 91130 is seen departing Peterborough while heading for London King's Cross. This loco now carries the name *Lord Mayor of Newcastle*, as well as 'Proudly Celebrating 800 Years of Newcastle's Mayoralty 1216–2016' underneath the plate and a silhouette of the Newcastle skyline above the plate.

No. 91130, 15 June 2017

No. 91130 *Lord Mayor of Newcastle* is seen arriving at Leeds with a Virgin Trains East Coast working from London King's Cross. Note that this loco, like the rest of the fleet, carries a forward-facing camera in the secondman's windscreen.

No. 91130, 15 June 2017

No. 91130 *Lord Mayor of Newcastle* arrives at Darlington. This shot was taken on the same day as the previous photograph at Leeds and just shows the large amount of mileage this particular class of locomotives accumulates, as the loco had been to London King's Cross and back in between the two photographs.

No. 91031, 5 April 1995

No. 91031 *Sir Henry Royce* is seen standing at London King's Cross carrying InterCity Swallow livery. This was the very last locomotive ever built at Crewe Works, who produced over 8,000 locomotives over 150 years, so it would make a fitting addition to the museum at York when its career has finished.

No. 91031, 30 March 1997

No. 91031 passes through Thirsk while propelling a GNER service to London King's Cross. During the early days of privatisation, it was common to see locomotives and stock carrying a mixture of liveries as the repainting process was ongoing.

No. 91031, 17 May 1997

No. 91031 stands at London King's Cross having arrived with a terminating GNER service. The loco is seen from its flush number two cab, again, unusually, facing south. The GNER blue livery was certainly a radical departure from the traditional InterCity Swallow livery at the time.

No. 91131, 13 August 2004

No. 91131 arrives at Doncaster, ready to make the station call. By this time the loco had been through the Project Delta refurbishment, emerging as No. 91131, and it is seen carrying the name *County of Northumberland*.

No. 91131, 19 September 2015

No. 91131 is seen departing from Edinburgh Waverley while propelling a Virgin Trains East Coast working to London King's Cross. The loco carries full Virgin Trains livery, but is starting to look scruffy on the front end, having lost some of the white. The two small holes underneath the windscreen are where the cleaners at London King's Cross used to place a ladder so they could give the windscreen a good clean in between trips.

No. 91131, 4 January 2016

No. 91131 races southbound through Peterborough while heading for London King's Cross. Peterborough has a bit of an unusual layout, with the Up fast being a platform line, whereas the Down fast, seen adjacent, is a through road.

No. 91131, 15 June 2017

No. 91131 is seen at Leeds having arrived with a terminating service. This locomotive holds the current speed record between London and Edinburgh, achieving it in just less than three and a half hours. This was achieved in 1991, with the loco achieving its maximum designed speed of 140 mph. The class offered so much potential on the East Coast without ever being given the chance to exploit it.